BUILDING SCIENCE

by Barbara Fierman

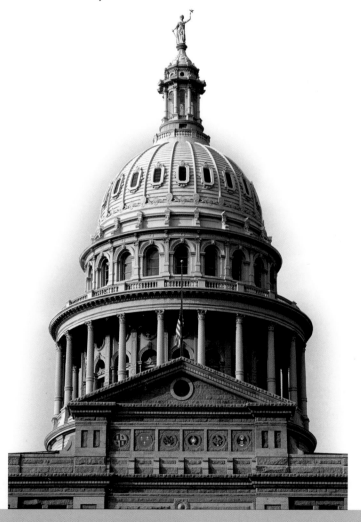

PEARSON

Scott
Foresman

What You Already Know

There are several different kinds of motion. Earth has a constant, or steady, motion as it moves around the Sun. Moving vehicles, such as cars, trucks, and buses, have variable motion, as they can move in many directions and at many different speeds. A pendulum has periodic motion as it swings back and forth. Wheels have circular motion as they turn round and round. A guitar string has a vibrational motion when it is plucked.

Average speed tells how far an object moves during a certain amount of time. Velocity describes the speed and the direction of an object's motion.

A force is a push or pull that acts on an object. Forces make a moving object speed up, slow down, change direction, or stop moving.

Gravity, magnetic forces, and electric forces can act between objects even if the objects do not touch. All three forces grow stronger as objects get closer together. Magnetism is a force that pushes and pulls on certain metals. Electric forces act between objects that are electrically charged.

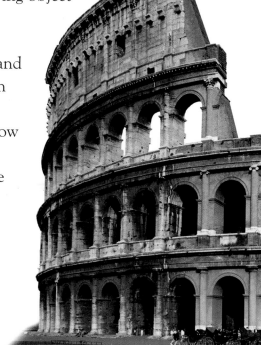

Buildings must be built to withstand many forces.

Work is the energy used when a force moves an object. Power is the rate at which work is done. The faster work is done, the greater the power.

When equal forces act on an object in opposite directions, the forces are balanced. This is called equilibrium.

Newton's first law of motion says that unless a net force acts on an object, the object will remain in constant motion. The tendency of an object to resist any change in motion is known as inertia. Newton's second law of motion describes how acceleration, mass, and net force are related. Acceleration is the rate at which the velocity of an object changes over time. Newton's third law of motion states that when one object exerts a force on a second object, the second object exerts a force on the first object.

A machine is a device that changes the direction or the amount of force needed to do work. Simple machines include a wheel and axle, a pulley, an inclined plane, and a lever.

Many forces are at work all the time in buildings. Architects and builders must understand these forces to make buildings safe and durable. Let's find out how this is done.

Building Scientists

Have you ever stopped to watch as a building was being built in your town or city? It might have been a house, a barn, or an apartment building in your neighborhood. Or it might have been a hospital, a school, or a hockey rink. What interested you most about the building process? Was it the many workers, the huge hole being excavated in the ground, or the massive pieces of equipment?

Constructing a building is a complicated project involving many types of workers, a fleet of machines, and a variety of building materials. If you've ever watched the construction process, you know that it requires the work of many people. What you might not realize is how many people are involved in the planning stage of the construction process.

Before a building is constructed, the land must be surveyed, or measured and mapped, to find the best location for the building.

While some architects plan and design buildings on paper, many now use computers to create designs.

Long before the construction workers begin to dig, architects design the building. Architects consider how the building should look, as well as what special features it will have. They create a set of plans, called blueprints, for the building.

Surveyors determine exactly where a building will be built. After the land has been cleared, the surveyors measure and mark where the foundation should be dug. Engineers help make these decisions. They collect soil samples and test them to find out where the soil or rock is strong enough to support the building. Engineers also help decide the best materials for the building. They work to decide how the building should be built in order to follow the town or city's building laws.

Balancing Forces

Architects and engineers have to plan for natural forces that will affect a building. These natural forces include gravity and wind. Gravity pulls everything in a building toward the ground. This puts stress on the building's parts and on the ground beneath it.

Wind, hurricanes, and earthquakes also put force on a building. Strong winds can push and pull on a structure. Parts of the building stretch apart, squeeze together, or bend. The stretching action is called tension, and the squeezing action is called compression. Engineers use mathematical formulas to figure out the total wind force that buildings can withstand.

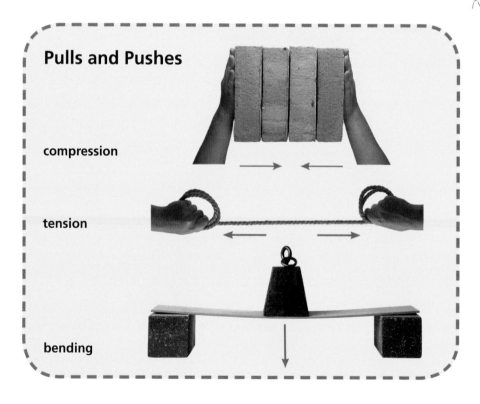

Pulls and Pushes

compression

tension

bending

If the forces are not balanced, the tent will collapse.

compression

tension

In this picture, yellow arrows represent compression forces, and red arrows represent tension.

A building has to be able to support its own weight and the weight of everything inside it. All of this weight pushes down through the building until it reaches the ground. This is called the building's load.

The forces on a building must be balanced, or the building will collapse. Look at the photo of the tent above. Gravity pushes down on the center pole with a compression force. If the pole were removed, the tent would fall down. There is tension on each of the tent's sides. If one side became detached from the ground, the tension on the other side would pull the tent over.

Firm Foundations

A strong foundation lets a building support itself and withstand the forces that pull and push on it. The foundation also gives a building a level base. The type of foundation a building needs depends on the type of soil or rock in the building site.

Scientists determine whether the ground is mainly solid rock, layers of different rocks, or soft soil. Next, an excavator, or digging machine, scoops dirt and rock from the place where the foundation will be built. The ground at the bottom of the hole is made level. Then concrete is poured to create a foundation.

A bulldozer levels the ground before a foundation is poured.

Buildings are extremely heavy and need strong foundations to support them.

When a skyscraper is constructed, footings, or concrete supports, are built into the ground. To make the footings, holes must be dug. Steel or wood forms are placed in the holes, and concrete is poured in. When the concrete hardens, the forms are removed. When soil freezes it expands, which can move footings. For this reason, footings reach deep into the ground, below the layer of soil that freezes in the winter.

Skyscrapers can also be built on concrete supports that are attached to solid bedrock deep in the earth. Long steel or concrete columns called piles are driven into the ground until they reach solid rock.

When a building is constructed on soft soil, a special type of foundation has to be built to spread out the building's weight. One way is to build a huge concrete slab for the building to rest on. A tower in Pisa, Italy, was built on soft soil without the right type of foundation. The soil under the building settled, and the tower began to tilt to one side. It is called the Leaning Tower of Pisa.

Strong Shapes

Some important shapes used in construction are the column, the arch, the dome, and the triangle. A column is a round, upright post that supports beams in a building. Columns were used in the construction of ancient buildings such as the Parthenon in Athens, Greece, and in more recent buildings such as the Lincoln Memorial in Washington, D.C.

An arch is a curved structure that forms the upper edge of an open space, such as a window or door. It supports the weight of the material above it by redirecting the force to the sides. When builders need to cover an open space such as a door or window opening, they place a beam called a lintel across the top. However, large spaces require very thick lintels. An arch is much stronger than a lintel, so arches can be built thinner and cover very large openings.

Building Forces

Some building shapes are stronger than others because of the way they spread out force.

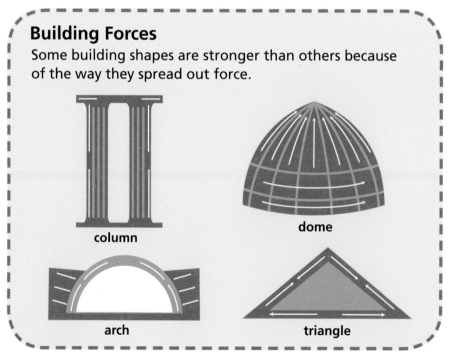

column

dome

arch

triangle

A dome is a curved roof that can create a huge open space. It acts similarly to many arches arranged in a circle. A dome supports its own load in addition to the load caused by wind, rain, snow, or ice. Many state capitols, and the U.S. Capitol in Washington, D.C., have domes.

A triangle is one of the strongest and most steady structures used in building construction. The triangular roof is sturdy, and its angles allow rainwater and snow to slide off rather than pile up, which could cause the roof to collapse under the weight.

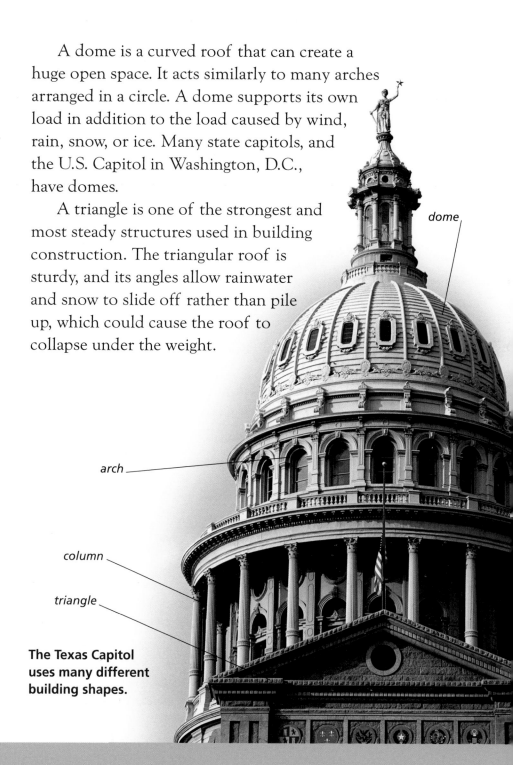

dome

arch

column

triangle

The Texas Capitol uses many different building shapes.

Stone Structures

Stone is one of the most widely used building materials. It is used for walls and steps of buildings and for supports of bridges. As a building material, stone is strong in compression. This means that the stone can resist forces that try to squeeze or crush it. Structures made from stone must be designed so that all the parts are pushed together by the weight of the stone.

Some of the oldest bridges in Europe are made of stone. An example is the Pont du Gard, pictured below. This bridge crosses the Gard River in France. It was built more than 2,000 years ago to carry water to the city of Nimes. It is 273 meters long and 49 meters high. This structure is held in place entirely by the weight of its stones. No mortar was used to hold it together.

Structures made of stone can last for thousands of years. The pyramids in Egypt were constructed thousands of years ago and still exist today. For example, the Great Pyramids of Giza are more than 4,500 years old!

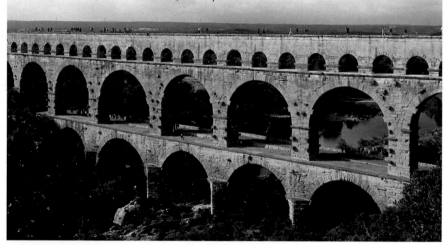

The ancient Pont du Gard is now used to carry cars.

The types of stone commonly used in construction are granite, limestone, sandstone, marble, and slate. Granite is a strong, hard type of stone, which makes it a good building material. It is resistant to the weather, but its hardness makes it difficult to cut.

Weather can wear away limestone.

Limestone and sandstone can be cut easily, but they are also easily worn away by wind and rain. Marble is a beautiful type of stone used to make monuments. Slate is often split into flat slabs and used for roof shingles and floors.

One advantage of stone as a building material is that it is fire resistant. In well-constructed buildings, stone can also be earthquake resistant. A disadvantage is that structures made of stone can take a long time to build.

After 4,500 years these pyramids are still some of the largest stone structures in the world.

Building with Brick

Another example of a strong construction material is brick. Bricks are long lasting and easy to produce in large quantities. They are usually made in standard sizes, which makes them much easier to work with than blocks of stone, which may be irregular. Like stone, bricks are strong in compression.

Bricks have been used in construction for thousands of years. In parts of Africa and Asia where the climate is hot and wood is scarce, people built houses of bricks. The first bricks were made of clay or mud, which were formed into blocks and dried in the Sun.

In 1666 a great fire destroyed many of the wood buildings in London, England. As a result many of the buildings constructed after the fire were made of brick to make them fire resistant. Native Americans of the southwestern United States built homes with a type of brick known as adobe. In cities brick was often used to pave streets until concrete replaced it in the 1900s.

Bricks

Bricks are held together with mortar. Mortar is a mixture of sand, water, and cement that becomes hard. To create a strong structure, bricks in one row overlap the spaces between the bricks on the row below.

Today, bricks are made of clay mixed with sand. They are formed by machines and baked in a special oven.

Higher quality bricks are used on the inside and outside walls of buildings, where appearance is important. These facing, or face, bricks are made from special types of clay. Lesser quality bricks, which may be uneven or have defects, are used in areas where they cannot be seen. They are called common bricks, and they are not specially treated for color or texture.

Many buildings in cities are built of brick.

Working with Wood

Wood is a light and strong construction material. It is easy to cut and shape and is often less expensive than other building materials. Where trees are plentiful, entire houses are made of wood. In other areas, houses may have a wood frame only. Even stone and brick houses may be partly made of wood.

Early settlers in the United States built log houses, which were constructed entirely of wood. Many of the parts of these houses were held together with wooden pegs. Flat pieces of wood were used for the roof, and floors might be made of logs that were split in half and placed with the flat side up.

Wood is a versatile building material.

Wood-frame houses have been built for hundreds of years. This type of construction is still in use today.

There are many different types of wood that can be used for buildings. Houses can be made from the wood of fir, pine, and spruce trees. The wood from oak, maple, walnut, and birch trees is used for features inside a house, such as stairways, cabinets, and floors.

There are some disadvantages to using wood as a construction material. Wood is not as strong as materials such as stone. When wood is exposed to weather, it can rot. Insects such as termites and carpenter ants can destroy wood. Wood also burns more easily than other building materials.

Steel Constructions

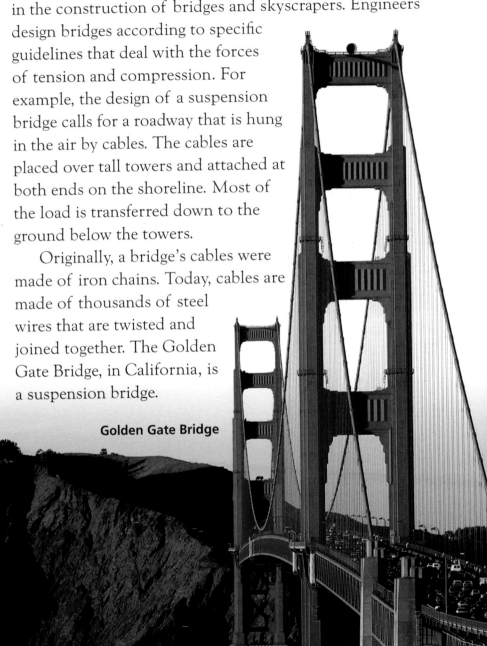

Steel is one of the most important building materials used in the construction of bridges and skyscrapers. Engineers design bridges according to specific guidelines that deal with the forces of tension and compression. For example, the design of a suspension bridge calls for a roadway that is hung in the air by cables. The cables are placed over tall towers and attached at both ends on the shoreline. Most of the load is transferred down to the ground below the towers.

Originally, a bridge's cables were made of iron chains. Today, cables are made of thousands of steel wires that are twisted and joined together. The Golden Gate Bridge, in California, is a suspension bridge.

Golden Gate Bridge

The first bridge built primarily of steel, the Firth of Forth Bridge in Scotland, was completed in 1890. It is one of the largest cantilever bridges ever built. A cantilever bridge uses a system of angled supports to spread out a load. About fifty-four thousand tons of steel were used in the bridge's construction. It is one of the strongest bridges ever built—even the strongest winds hardly shake it.

Skyscrapers are constructed of steel columns connected to horizontal steel beams. The beams and columns are bolted and welded together. Concrete floors rest on the beams.

Very tall buildings would not be possible without steel beams.

Steel Bridges

Cantilever bridges use steel girders to support tension and compression. By creating a pattern of triangles, they are extremely strong. Suspension bridges use steel cables to hold the roadway in place. The cables can withstand very strong tension.

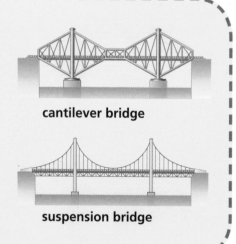

cantilever bridge

suspension bridge

Using Concrete

Concrete is a durable building material that is used for a wide variety of purposes. Since concrete is so strong, it is good for making foundations for buildings. It is also used to keep posts or poles for flags, fences, or swing sets fixed in the ground. Since it can form a hard, flat, and durable surface, it is used for roads, sidewalks, and airport runways. Airplanes easily roll across a concrete runway.

Since concrete is a waterproof material, it can be used in the construction of dams, canals, and underground water pipes. The largest concrete dam is the Grand Coulee Dam in Washington State. Twelve million cubic feet of concrete were used in the dam's construction.

The Colosseum in Rome was partially made from concrete.

Many modern buildings are constructed with concrete.

The ancient Romans first used concrete for buildings, bridges, and roads thousands of years ago. Because concrete is such a long-lasting material, many of these structures still exist today. Ancient Roman concrete contained limestone, water, and volcanic ash. Today, concrete is made of a mixture of sand, water, and gravel held together by limestone and clay. It can be reinforced with steel, which makes it even stronger.

In addition to being strong and durable, concrete is also easy to care for. Unlike wood structures, concrete structures don't have to be painted. Concrete doesn't rot or rust. Concrete can be poured into almost any shape, so it is used to build many interesting-looking, modern buildings.

Reinforced Concrete
Reinforced concrete combines steel with concrete to make a strong material that is used for many large buildings.

Built to Last

In many parts of the world, hurricanes and earthquakes destroy or severely damage buildings. In these areas architects and engineers are working to design buildings that can withstand these natural forces.

Many buildings are unable to withstand earthquakes.

Some of the elements designers are focusing on include the shape of the building and the materials used to construct it. They must also consider how close it will be to other buildings and what type of soil it will be built on.

In an earthquake, movements in the ground cause a building's foundation to vibrate from side to side. If a building can bend with the movement, it is less likely to be damaged. Skyscrapers constructed of steel and concrete are able to move fairly well. Engineers sometimes put flexible rubber pads between a building and the ground. This protects the building by reducing the amount of vibrations that reach it.

The Transamerica Pyramid in San Francisco is earthquake resistant.

Architects and engineers think about many things when they design new buildings. They have learned which materials are stronger than others, as well as how to use combinations of materials to make them even stronger. They have learned which shapes are better able to support loads. They have developed ways to provide strong foundations even in areas where the soil is soft.

As architects and engineers learn more about the effects of hurricanes and earthquakes on buildings, they will be better able to improve their designs. As time goes by, buildings will become bigger, stronger, and safer.

Glossary

architect　　　　　a person who designs buildings and other structures

blueprints　　　　drawings that show the design of a building

compression　　　a force that presses things together

footing　　　　　underground support, usually made of concrete, on which columns or walls can be set

form　　　　　　a wooden or metal mold used to hold wet concrete while it sets

foundation　　　the solid base under a building

pile　　　　　　a concrete column reaching down to solid rock under layers of soft soil

reinforced concrete　　a very strong concrete that contains steel rods or wires

surveyor　　　　a person who measures a building site to make sure that everything is in the correct position

tension　　　　　a force that pulls or stretches